ARTIST-IN-TRAINING

You Can Paint Like the Masters

by Amy Runyen
and the Creative Team at Walter Foster

Table of Contents

Introduction

In this book, you'll learn how to re-create your very own masterpieces step by step, while gaining an understanding of art history. As you follow the lessons in this book, be sure to read the brief biographies—these will help you learn about art history and acrylic painting techniques.

The projects in this book do not use the exact techniques that these artists would have used to create their artwork. Instead, the lessons show you how to create your own paintings that resemble famous artworks using easy-to-follow directions.

Most of the artwork in this book would have been originally painted in oil, but this book uses acrylic paint because it is easy to apply, and you just need a little water and a brush to paint with it.

Enjoy your painting journey!

Timeline

As you complete the projects in this book, return to these pages to see where the artwork fits in history!

1889:
Van Gogh paints
The Starry Night

1914:
Monet paints
Water Lilies

1890:
Cézanne paints
Pine Tree Near Aix

1913:
Kandinski paints
Squares with Concentric Circles

1873:
Monet paints
Poppy Fields

1850   1860   1870   1880   1890   1900   1910

1872:
Monet paints
Regatta at Argenteuil

1888:
Van Gogh paints
Bedroom at Arles

1890:
Van Gogh paints *Irises*

c. 1900:
Cézanne paints
Still Life with Milk Jug and Fruit

1889:
Van Gogh paints *Sunflowers*

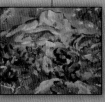

c. 1900:
Cézanne paints
Mont Sainte-Victoire

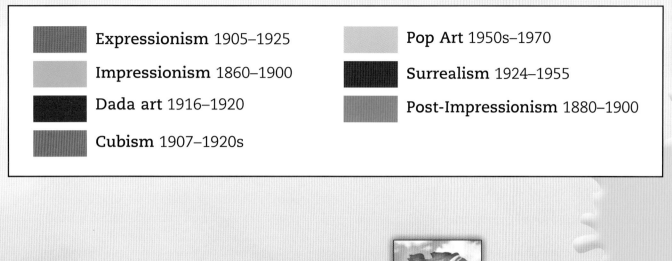

Expressionism 1905–1925

Impressionism 1860–1900

Dada art 1916–1920

Cubism 1907–1920s

Pop Art 1950s–1970

Surrealism 1924–1955

Post-Impressionism 1880–1900

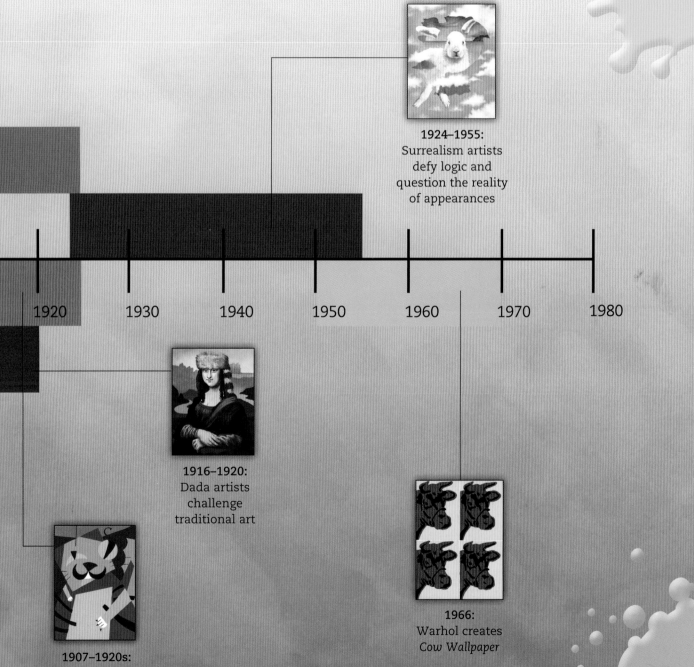

1924–1955:
Surrealism artists
defy logic and
question the reality
of appearances

1920   1930   1940   1950   1960   1970   1980

1916–1920:
Dada artists
challenge
traditional art

1966:
Warhol creates
Cow Wallpaper

1907–1920s:
Picasso and Braque
develop Cubism

5

Tools & Materials

Before you start the projects in this book, look over these pages and make sure you have everything you need!

Acrylic Paints

To re-create the projects in this book, you'll need the following paint colors: crimson, violet, burnt umber, phthalo blue, cobalt blue, lemon yellow, yellow ochre, light green, black, and white. Sometimes you'll use a color straight from the tube; other times you'll mix colors together or add water to your paints to create lighter, thinner applications of color. For more on color mixing, see pages 8–9.

Paintbrushes

For the projects in this book, you'll need two paintbrushes: one flat brush and one round brush. Flat brushes are good for filling in large areas of color, whereas round brushes have a smaller tip and are great for painting details. When using acrylic paint, it's best to use brushes with synthetic bristles. Be sure to rinse out your brushes with water in between colors! And, to keep your brushes in good condition, wash them with mild soap and water when you're finished painting.

Painting Surfaces

You can apply acrylic paint over paper or canvas (just make sure your canvas is pre-primed). The best paper to use is thick watercolor paper, which won't buckle or warp too much when you apply the paint.

Mixing Palette

Mixing palettes are helpful tools for mixing and thinning colors. They generally come with several wells for holding different colors. And it's easy to clean a plastic palette using plain soap and warm water. If you don't have a palette, a disposable plastic plate will work.

Plastic Palette Knife

A palette knife has two uses: mixing colors and applying paint. You can use a plastic palette knife to mix colors on your palette without dirtying your brush. Or you can use it to apply thick strokes of paint to your artwork!

Extra Materials

In addition to the tools shown on this page, you'll also want to gather the following before you begin: two jars of water (one for rinsing your brush and one for thinning your acrylic paint), paper towels, a pencil for transferring your sketches (see page 12), and transfer paper (see page 12 again).

7

Color Mixing

There are many different ways to approach painting, which is why there are so many artistic styles. But artists of every style will agree on one thing: Color is one of the most important parts of a painting. Learning the basics about colors and how to mix them won't guarantee you fame in the art world—but it will make you a better artist!

The Color Wheel

The color wheel illustrates relationships between colors. The primary colors—red, yellow, and blue—can't be created by mixing other colors. If you mix two primaries, you'll get a secondary color—orange, green, and purple. Mixing a primary with a secondary produces a tertiary color (such as red-orange or blue-green). Half the colors (red, orange, and yellow) are considered "warm." The other half (green, blue, and purple) are considered "cool." Warm colors are often thought of as energetic and exciting, whereas cool colors are considered more relaxed and calming.

Mixing Colors

Mixing two colors together creates a third color. For example, red plus yellow makes orange. But you can create many different colors by varying the amounts of the colors in your mixes, as shown at right. When you mix equal parts of two colors, you get one result. But when you mix "a little" or "a dot" of one color into another, the result is very different!

Mixing Browns and Neutrals

To produce a brown or a gray, called a "neutral" color, you'll need to mix two or more colors together. Browns are usually a combination of the three primary colors, whereas most grays are a mix of complements (colors opposite each other on the color wheel). You can also mix white and black to make gray. At right, each primary and secondary color has been mixed with its complement. When you mix browns using complements, the result is called a "chromatic gray."

Lightening a Color with Water

You can lighten any color by adding water; this mixture is called a "wash." The more water you add, the lighter the color will become—and the thinner the paint will be. Below, pure burnt umber (straight from the tube) is shown on the far left. In each example to the right, more and more water has been added to lighten the color.

Creating Tints

You can also lighten any color by adding white paint, which will produce a thicker paint mixture, more opaque mixture than lightening with water will. The more white you add, the lighter the color will be. Below, white has been added to each primary color.

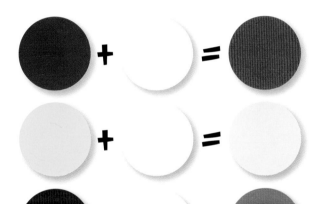

Creating Shades

You can darken any color by adding a little black paint. The more black you add, the darker the color will become. As you can see below, black has been added to each primary color.

Desaturating

One way to desaturate a color is to mix it with gray. (A color plus gray is called a "tone.") Desaturating dulls a color to create a softer, more muted version. Experiment and discover the range of colors you can create by mixing gray with each of your paints. You might be surprised at how many tones are possible!

Acrylic Techniques

Use these basics techniques throughout your paintings.

Flat Wash

Wet your paper with clear water and then load a flat brush with thinned paint. Starting at the top, pull the color from left to right and work down to the bottom.

Gradation

Apply a wash, but add more water between each stroke so that the color gradually fades or gets lighter. This is good for painting skies and water.

Impasto

Use the paint straight from the tube and apply thick layers of paint with your brush or palette knife to add ridges of texture.

Using the Palette Knife

By applying paint to the paper or canvas with a palette knife, you can create textured areas that are good for highlights.

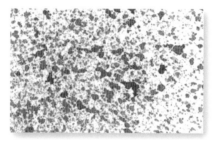

Spattering

Load an old toothbrush with paint and run your thumb over the bristles to release a spray of dots on your painting.

Drybrush

Dip the tip of a damp brush in thick paint and lightly wipe it on a paper towel; drag the brush onto dry paper or a dry color.

Scumbling

Use a dry brush to apply a new color over already-dry paint, moving the brush in a gentle, circular motion.

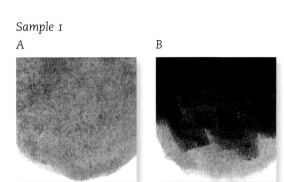

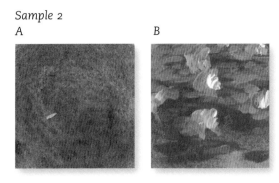

Underpainting or Tone Wash

Many artists start their paintings by covering the paper or canvas with a thin wash of color, called an "underpainting" or a "tone wash." This first layer of paint serves as a base or foundation on which you can build colors. In many of the projects, you will begin by applying thin washes of color (sample 1A) based on your template. The underpainting prevents little bits of white paper from showing through your brushstrokes when you apply thicker layers of paint (sample 1B). For another example of this type of underpainting, see the project on page 16.

In other projects, you'll start with a wash of one color—usually a neutral such as brown (sample 2A). This tone wash will help unify all the colors in your final painting. Sometimes you'll want the underpainting to peek through in areas for interest, as in the grass above (sample 2B). For another example of this type of underpainting, see the project on page 22.

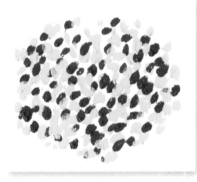

Stippling

Stippling is applying a series of small dots to create the appearance of texture or to optically blend color—this means that the colors aren't really blended, but they appear to be when viewed from far away. Dab on color in short, circular motions, holding the brush very straight. Try overlapping and layering the dots as shown at far right—when you look at it from a distance, the dots seem to blend together to create a new color.

Using the Templates

Each project in this book comes with a template
located at the back of the book (see page 78).

Templates

The templates in this book will allow you to transfer the main guidelines of each painting to your paper or canvas. This way you don't have to draw anything—you can just paint! Begin by making a photocopy of the template. Then all you have to do is transfer the lines and you can get started using acrylic paint!

Using Transfer Paper

The simplest way to transfer the lines is to use transfer paper, which you can buy at your local arts and crafts store. Transfer paper is a thin sheet of paper that is coated on one side with graphite—the same material that makes up the "lead" of drawing pencils. The following steps will help you put your transfer paper to good use.

Step 1 Place the transfer paper over your painting surface. Once you have the copy of the template, place it on top of the transfer paper and hold it in place with masking tape.

Step 2 Then lightly trace over the lines of the template with a pencil or the handle of a paintbrush. As you trace, the lines will transfer to your painting surface! Use light pressure when tracing the sketch, as you don't want to leave marks on your paper or canvas.

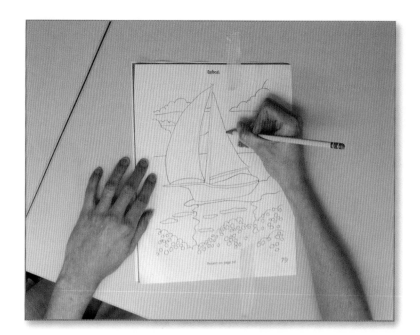

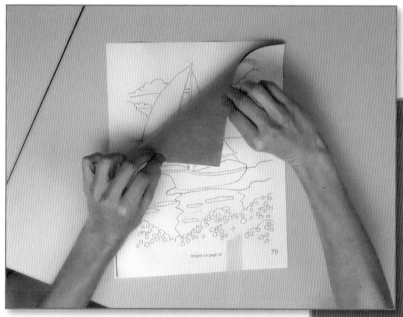

Step 3 While tracing the lines of the template, occasionally lift the corner of the template and the transfer paper to make sure that the lines aren't too dark. Continue tracing until all of the lines have transferred to your painting surface.

Make Your Own Transfer Paper

If you can't get transfer paper at your art store, simply make your own! First make a photocopy of the template and use a pencil to completely cover the back of the photocopy with graphite, pressing down hard to create an even layer.

Paint Like an Impressionist!

The *Impressionists* were a group of artists in the late 1800s who began painting with a never-before-used method. Instead of mixing their paints on a palette to create colors, these painters applied colors straight to the canvas in small strokes and dashes. The viewer's eye would then visually blend the different strokes of color, giving the impression of a new color. The Impressionists also focused on painting light and the variations of color within it. There are rarely hard edges or solid areas of color in Impressionist paintings, which gives them a softer look. These paintings show delicate impressions of the objects rather than photolike re-creations.

Turn to page 16 to paint a masterpiece in the style of an Impressionist!

Playing with Light and Color

Creating Colors on the Canvas

Impressionists have a unique way of applying paint to the canvas. For example, to paint a peach, a traditional artist would mix several shades and variations of peach colors and apply them to the canvas (below left). But an Impressionist might not premix peach paint colors; instead, the artist would apply very small strokes of red, pink, orange, and yellow next to one another (below right). The separate strokes of colors visually blend when you step back from the painting, producing more intense shades and a better imitation of the way natural light shimmers.

Painting with Quick Strokes

The Impressionists painted with very quick strokes to record the light and color of a scene and to suggest movement. Because Earth is constantly rotating, natural light is always moving and changing—from sunrise to sunset. And the colors and light at sunrise and sunset aren't constant either; essentially, the Impressionists wanted to capture their impression of a fleeting moment in time. A scene painted with smooth, blended strokes (below left) isn't as lively as one done with short, feathery strokes (below right).

Sailboat

Paint a sailboat in the style
of the Impressionists!

Step 1 Begin your painting with very thin
washes of color. For a soft, Impressionist
look, cover each shape with water before
applying the colored washes. Called
"painting wet into wet," this technique
creates smooth, even blocks of color.

Transfer the sketch on page 79!!

Step 2 When the first washes are dry,
use a dry brush with a little paint to dab
on darker colors. The dry brush creates
texture, and it leaves gaps where the lighter
colors can show through. For the hills, use
light green; for the sky and water, mix a
little phthalo blue into white.

Step 3 Continue developing the darker colors of
the painting by dabbing on thick paint in short
strokes, always letting spots of the lighter colors
peek through. Finish the dark blue of the sky and
the green of the hills; then build up the greens in the
foreground shrubs. Use crimson and burnt umber for
the ship's accents. For the lake, mix white with a dot
each of black and phthalo blue. Dab the paint over
the lake, giving the water a sense of movement.

Step 4 Now add your lightest and brightest colors, stroking with a quick dabbing motion to add the bright flowers, greens of the foliage, and white highlights on the water. You don't have to render each shape perfectly—use small dabs of color to give the viewer the impression of the subject.

Water Lilies

"It took me time to understand my waterlilies. I had planted them for the pleasure of it; I grew them without ever thinking of painting them." — Claude Monet

Transfer the sketch on page 80!

Step 1 Begin by painting over the entire paper with a water-thinned mossy green mix made of light green, lemon yellow, and burnt umber. Use a flat brush to apply the wash, stroking from left to right and working from top to bottom. (You can repeat this step if the underpainting appears too light at first.)

Step 2 Fill in the darker green areas of the background, applying short, vertical strokes. Then paint the lighter green portions of the background in the same manner, sometimes overlapping the darker areas. (Building up the color helps create a sense of depth and dimension in the finished piece.)

Step 3 Mix a new green to paint the shadowed areas underneath and around the lily flowers, making oval outlines to start defining the flowers. Then mix equal parts of the new green with the dark green from step two to paint vertical strokes throughout the painting and to soften the edges of the flower shadows.

Step 4 Use vertical strokes to apply a blue mix of cobalt blue, white, violet, and burnt umber to the bright areas of the water. Create harmony in the painting by tying the color into the flowers too, making small ovals of color in places and partial oval outlines in others, as shown.

Step 5 Fill in the aqua portions of the water by making vertical strokes with a mix of cobalt blue, lemon yellow, and white. Switch to a blue mix of white, cobalt blue, and lemon yellow to paint circular swatches on the lily pads, creating a base for the lilies themselves.

Step 6 Swirl a round brush in a circular motion to apply a purple mix of white, violet, and burnt umber to the lilies, as shown. Then mix white with lemon yellow and burnt umber to paint the "white" areas of the flowers in the same manner. Don't be concerned about detail or blending!

Step 7 Mix a dark red to swirl colorful accents into the lilies, as shown. Then mix lemon yellow with white for the flowers' yellow swirls and accents. To finish, fill in the darkest shadows; use a circular stroke to apply a rich, near-black mix of violet, burnt umber, and light green.

Poppy Fields

"Everyone discusses my art and pretends to understand, as if it were necessary to understand, when it is simply necessary to love." — Claude Monet

Transfer the sketch on page 81!

Step 1 For the background color, make a thin wash by adding a lot of water to pure yellow ochre. Use a flat brush to apply the wash, stroking from top to bottom and working from left to right until the entire paper is covered. This color will peek through subsequent layers.

Step 2 Mix equal amounts of cobalt blue and white to paint the upper, dark areas of the sky. Then keep adding more white to the mix as you move down toward the horizon, blending where different blue mixtures meet. As you paint, soften the edges around the areas you've painted with a dry brush.

Step 3 Mix a cream color to fill in the clouds. Then drybrush the edges, working your brush into the blue to create fluffy clouds. Add more yellow ochre and burnt umber to the mix to drybrush over the clouds on the left. Then paint in the foreground greens with a mix of equal parts light green and yellow ochre..

Step 4 Scumble pure white highlights in the clouds. With a dark green mix, paint the row of trees, softening the edges with a dry brush. Add more light green and yellow ochre to the mix; then paint over the darker grass, blending with the previously applied green. Fill the remaining grass with a light green mix, using drybrush and wet-on-wet techniques to blend the transitions.

Step 5 Use the light green from step four to create "halos" around a few tree tops. Blend accents in the grass with a light brown mix and short vertical strokes. Paint the large treetop with the same mix. Add darks to the trees with the dark green mix. Then fill the wall of the house with beige. Use the medium green from step four to touch in dark grass near the figures.

Step 6 For the poppies, add a touch of violet to red. Use a peach color (white, yellow, and red) for the figures' skin, mixing a dot of tan with a dot of burnt umber for hat and chin shadows. Apply the step five dark green to the house windows. Mix brown for the figure's skirt, adding blue and white to the mix for the blouse. With a green mix, paint the children's shirts. Drybrush a gray mix into the landscape.

Step 7 Paint the lighter portions of the poppies with a red-orange mix. Add more white to the mix as you work toward the background, and add a touch of yellow ochre to paint the roof of the house and the red band on the boy's hat. With a mix of equal parts burnt umber and violet, paint the hair and clothing, as shown. Use a blue mix to fill in the parasol.

Project based on *Poppy Fields* (1873) by Claude Monet.

Step 8 Mix a dot of the step seven blue with a bit of burnt umber for the shadow in the parasol. Add a hint of white to the blue for the parasol's highlight. Use pure yellow ochre for the handle. Mix a yellow to dot in the distant yellow flowers, adding a hint of darker yellow for the closer ones. Mix equal parts yellow ochre and white to paint the figures' hats to finish.

Regatta at Argenteuil

"These landscapes of water and reflection
have become an obsession." —Claude Monet

Transfer the sketch on page 82!

Step 1 Mix a light brown color to cover the entire background with a solid wash. Use a flat brush to apply the color to the paper in long, overlapping strokes. And be sure to add plenty of water to your paint mix so that it flows smoothly from your brush.

Step 2 Now create a thick application of blue by mixing cobalt blue, white, and burnt umber. Use a flat brush to apply the color to the darkest areas of the sky and water, as shown. (Be sure to rinse your brush between colors to prevent your colors from becoming flat or muddied in appearance.)

Step 3 Create a second blue mix for the lighter areas of the sky and water, again applying the color with your flat brush. As you paint, use your brush to blend the light and dark areas together where they meet. And sweep some of the lighter blue color into the dark areas for variety and movement.

Step 4 Add a little white to the blue mix from step three to paint the lightest areas of the sky and water. Then mix equal parts white and lemon yellow to paint the sail on the left and its reflection. Touch some of this color on the house, bushes, and water, as shown. Add an equal part of white to the yellow mix to paint the remainder of the sails and their reflections.

Step 5 With a green mix, paint the darkest areas of the foliage on the river bank, along with a few reflections in the water. Then apply an orange mix over the main part of the houses and their reflections. Use a round brush and a red mix to create the darker accents on the houses, as well as their corresponding reflections.

Step 6 Mix a dark green to fill in the grass and trees, as shown. Then stroke reflections in the water. Next add yellow ochre to the mix for the light green portions of the trees and the corresponding reflections, and use your brush to blend the two greens in places. Mix a new orange color for the front of the house on the left and the windows of the house on the right.

Step 7 For the neutral green portions of the horizon (behind the boats and a little in the water and sky), mix white, yellow ochre, and cobalt blue. Then mix a brighter green for the boat on the right side of the painting. Add a little more lemon yellow to the bright green to touch in highlights in the foliage. And use pure white to drybrush highlights on the center boat and in the sky.

Step 8 Pick up a mix of equal parts burnt umber and yellow ochre to paint all the brown accents that you see, including the figures on the boat and the reflections. Switch to pure burnt umber for dark brown accents. Then add pure yellow ochre accents to the ship masts. For the final touch, mix a yellow for accents on the people, the water, and the house on the left.

Paint Like a Post-Impressionist!

Unlike other art movements that are associated with a specific style, *Post-Impressionism* is more of a time period. Painters of this movement were influenced by the Impressionist painters, but they took the basic ideas of Impressionism and expanded on them. These painters had their own individual ways of using Impressionism to develop a unique style. One of the most famous Post-Impressionists, Vincent Van Gogh, is known for his bright colors, bold strokes, and emotional paintings. On the following pages, you'll learn how to apply rich colors of paint in swirls and thick strokes to imitate Van Gogh's lively method of painting!

Turn to page 32 to paint this Post-Impressionist masterpiece!

Playing with Strokes

Creating Movement

Van Gogh conveyed a sense of energy and movement in his paintings—some people even say that his paintings of trees and flowers appear as though they're on fire! He created this impression by using small dashes of color, arranging the paint into vibrant curving or swirling patterns. When you look at his painting, your eyes follow these designs as the strokes guide them throughout the painting. These bold strokes can transform a simple star (below left) into a work of art (below right)!

Using Impasto

Van Gogh didn't just paint in small dashes—he also gave some of his paintings a 3-D look by applying the paint very thickly, creating a bumpy texture. This technique is called "impasto." With impasto, you can apply thick globs of paint with either your brush or your palette knife. For a spiky texture, try pressing down on the wet paint with your knife and then lifting straight up off the paper! As you compare the two images below, note the way that the impasto stokes on the poppy on the right have given the flower personality!

Sunflowers

"What would life be like if we had no courage to attempt anything?"
—Vincent van Gogh

Transfer the sketch on page 83!

Step 1 Begin with very thin washes of color. Paint the sunflowers with light yellow and orange (mix yellow and crimson), the stems with light green, and the vase with yellow and light gray (lighten black with water). Outline the vase with a little bit of orange. And don't forget to add burnt umber to the centers of the flowers!

Step 2 Next fill in the background with a wash of light blue-green. (Mix phthalo blue, white, a little green, and water.) Then color the tabletop with a wash of orange-yellow. Once you've covered the paper with washes, you'll have a basic guideline, or map, for your later colors.

Step 3 Now add darker colors. Fill in the background with a light blue-green color made by mixing white, phthalo blue, and a dot of green. When this dries, create a slightly lighter mix by adding white; then apply thick, impasto brushstrokes to the background. Next paint the sunflowers with an orange mixed from yellow and burnt umber, and paint the tabletop with a slightly lighter color. Use green to paint the stems, and use yellow and white to paint the vase. Add a few highlights to the vase using thick white paint.

Step 4 Finish with a few details. Apply thick strokes of light orange to the tabletop. Then use different shades of orange and yellow to create the petals on the flowers, and add a few fun swirls to the centers of the sunflowers. Next outline sections of the stems with black, and then outline the vase and tabletop with a mix of crimson and burnt umber. To finish, add a few more white highlights to the vase.

The Starry Night

"There may be a great fire in our soul, and no one ever comes to warm himself at it; the passers-by see only a little bit of smoke coming through the chimney, and then pass on their way." —Vincent van Gogh

Transfer the sketch on page 84!

Step 1 Begin by painting over the entire paper with a water-thinned blue-green mix made of phthalo blue, burnt umber, and light green. Use a flat brush to apply the wash, stroking from top to bottom and working from left to right. (You can repeat this step if the underpainting appears too light at first.)

Step 2 Use the edge of your brush and short, dashlike strokes to apply the dark blue mix into the sky. Use a dark olive mix of light green, burnt umber, white, and dark yellow to fill in areas of the foreground and the stairway in front of the village. Add more white and yellow to the mix for the lighter areas shown.

Step 3 Fill the mountains using a mix of phthalo blue, white, and burnt umber; stroke in the direction of the mounded shape. Apply dashes of the same mix in the grass and sky. Add a little white to the blue mix from step two for dashes in the sky. Then dash a cream mix into the sky as well.

Step 4 Mix white and dark yellow to make little yellow dashes around the moon and stars. Then mix a gray using the green from step two, phthalo blue, and white. Dash this color through the sky and village to unify the painting. Mix a dot of white into phthalo blue and add a small amount of crimson to paint a few rooftops.

Step 5 Using dark yellow with a hint of white, paint the moon and flecks on some stars. Add a hint of crimson to the mix for the orange points of the moon and some stars. Mix white, phthalo blue, and dark yellow for the turquoise flecks around the moon, stars, and swirl; in the bushes; and on the rooftops.

Step 6 Mix light green with burnt umber and yellow to fill the cypress trees; then add accents to the village. Create a dark blue mix of phthalo blue with a dot of white and a little black to add more darks to the village. Add a bit of the green mix to the dark blue for the homes. Use black to define lines between the buildings.

Step 7 For the tree's lines, mix a reddish brown using burnt umber, crimson, and dark yellow. Use expressive brushstrokes that curve and flow freely, without following the sketch exactly. Switch to dark yellow for the village's interior lights. Mix in a hint of crimson for lights with an orange glow.

Step 8 Use pure black for final house and bush outlines, extreme shadows, and curvy texture lines on the cypress tree. (You may want to water down the black so it flows more easily.) Add a little white to the halo around the moon and apply white dashes to the bright star near the cypress.

Bedroom at Arles

"This time it's just simply my bedroom, only here color is to do everything, and giving by its simplification a grander style to things, is to be suggestive here of rest or of sleep in general. In a word, looking at the picture ought to rest the brain, or rather imagination." —Vincent van Gogh

Transfer the sketch on page 85!

Step 1 For the background color, make a thin wash by adding a lot of water to a mixture of burnt umber, crimson, and phthalo blue with a dot of white. Use a flat brush to apply the wash, stroking from top to bottom and working from left to right until the entire paper is covered. This color will peek through subsequent layers.

Step 2 Paint the back wall and the doors using vertical strokes of a medium blue mix. Add white to the mix for the light blue side walls. Paint the floor boards with a brown wash. Switch to a green mix for the window panes. Then fill the doors with a dark blue mix. Mix orange to paint the nightstand.

Step 3 Apply a dark brown to the floor, occasionally touching in the orange and green mixes from step two. The window frame is light green accented with burnt umber. Dark yellow and white lighten the orange for nightstand accents. The towel, mirror, and doorframe are light brown with burnt umber darks.

Step 4 Mix a dark yellow for the chair. Then use the lightened orange from step three to paint the coat rack and hat. Add a hint of burnt umber to the mix for defining lines. For the hanging picture, apply the chair color to the frame, the green mix from step two to the grass, and the light brown from step three to the sky. Begin the portraits using other previously mixed colors.

Step 5 Fill in some clothes using the blue mixes from step two. For the vase and pitcher, use the medium blue from step two. For the brush and soap, use the towel browns from step three. For the papers on the walls, mix equal parts dark yellow and white; "draw" with burnt umber. For the blue-green of the portrait on the left, add a hint of phthalo blue to the green from step two.

Step 6 Mix a little phthalo blue and white to outline the vase, pitcher, cup, and clothing. (It's okay to mix this color freely without worrying about matching exactly.) Mix a yellow for the dark side of the bed frame; paint thickly, making big, clumpy streaks, and stroke in the direction of the sketch lines, adding touches of crimson occasionally

Step 7 Add white to the yellow from step six to paint the rest of the bed frame; accent with burnt umber. Use the original yellow to paint the far chair seat. Add dark yellow and light green for the near chair seat. Mix equal parts crimson and dark yellow for the far seat "X." Paint the covers red and creatm (white mixed with a dot of dark yellow), with white variation. Add burnt umber to the cream to "draw" pillows.

Project based on *Bedroom at Arles* (1888) by Vincent van Gogh.

Step 8 Use pure phthalo blue to line the doors, corners of the room, and window frame. Switch to pure burnt umber to outline the chairs, bed, mirror frame, hanging wire, nightstand, towel, and corners where the walls and the floor meet. (You may want to water down the paint into a wash so it flows from the paintbrush more easily.)

Irises

"But I always think that the best way to know God is to love many things."
—Van Gogh

Transfer the sketch on page 86!

Step 1 Cover the entire paper with a dark yellow wash. Create golden mixes of paint with yellow, adding small amounts of red and burnt umber. Use a flat brush to apply the golden yellow mixes to the background, making thick, impasto-style strokes and keeping the top of the painting darkest. Mix in a hint of white for the very light areas to the right of the flowers.

Step 2 Mix a dark orange color for the table, applying the color in the same thick method as you used to paint the background. Occasionally add little swatches of dark yellow and burnt umber as you work, providing variety.

Step 3 Mix a yellow for the vase, and apply the color with thick impasto strokes. Add a bit of white to your mix to paint the rim and vase handle. Then mix two greens for the leaves and stems. Begin painting the leaves and stems, as shown.

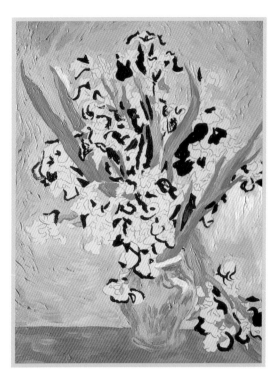

Step 4 Make yet another green mix to further develop the leaves and stems, as shown. Mix a little burnt umber into the yellow mix from step three. Stroke this mix and the orange from step two onto the vase for shape and dimension.

Step 5 Mix black with phthalo blue and a dot of white for the darkest areas of the flowers. Apply the color using the tip of a round brush to get into the small areas, as shown. As in the previous steps, apply the paint thickly, leaving behind visible brushstrokes.

Step 6 Next mix the two midtone blues, applying them to the flowers with thick strokes using the tip of a round brush. Following the example, place more of the lighter-colored mix to the left and center of the painting, toward the focal point.

Step 7 While the midtone blues are still wet, mix and a apply a blue for the lightest parts of the flowers. Let the colors blend and merge where they meet. Then mix a gray to fill in the neutral areas of the painting, as shown.

Project based on *Irises* (1890) by Vincent van Gogh.

Step 8 Use pure burnt umber to "draw" the outlines of the vase and table top. Switch to the blue mix from step five to outline the leaves, stems, and flowers, also touching up dark areas of the flowers. Mix a dingy yellow for the few visible pollen pieces.

Pine Tree Near Aix

"…I believe in the logical development of everything we see and feel through the study of nature…" —Paul Cézanne*

Transfer the sketch on page 87!

Step 1 Start by creating a wash with burnt umber and water. With a flat brush, paint the entire working area. Repeat this step if necessary to get a nice, even tone. This will give you a good foundation for your painting.

Step 2 With a flat brush and a mix of cobalt blue, white, and a dot of burnt umber, paint the dark areas of the sky. With a flat brush and a mix of violet, white, and dots of burnt umber and cobalt blue, stroke in the purple of the mountains seen through the trees.

Step 3 Mix white with dots of cobalt blue and burnt umber, and use a flat brush to paint the light blue areas of the sky, blending the patches of dark blue and violet where they meet. Don't be afraid to let the colors bleed into each other. Next create an orange by mixing yellow ochre with some dark yellow and crimson, and paint all the orange areas as shown.

* Chipp, Herschel B. *Theories of Modern Art*. Los Angeles: University of California Press, 1968, 22.

Step 4 Mix another orange with white, yellow ochre, dark yellow, and a dot of crimson, and paint this on top of the darker orange areas, allowing the colors to blend. Then add more white to this mix and paint the lighter orange areas, as shown. With white and dots of yellow ochre and dark yellow, paint the walls of the houses. Using white and dots of cobalt blue and yellow ochre, paint the highlights in the sky, blending the colors with the background.

Step 5 Using yellow ochre and a little crimson, paint the rooftops of the houses with a round brush. With a flat brush, use this color to place some accents throughout the painting, especially in the foreground. With a mix of light green, yellow ochre, and dots of dark yellow and crimson, use a flat brush to paint the grass around the tree trunk, painting in short vertical and horizontal strokes. With a mix of burnt umber and light green, paint the darker green areas.

Step 6 Use the burnt umber and light green mix from step 5 and a flat brush to paint the dark areas in the foreground with big, broad strokes. Paint the tree trunk and branches with a mix of violet and burnt umber. Then, using a round brush and a mix of burnt umber with a bit of yellow ochre and crimson, add the dark red accents to the foreground, allowing the new colors to blend with the surrounding colors.

Step 7 Use the burnt umber, yellow ochre, and crimson mix from step 6 to paint reddish highlights on the tree trunk and some of the branches. With the green, yellow ochre, dark yellow, and crimson mix from step 5, paint the midtones in the foreground. With cobalt blue, green, and a dot of yellow ochre, paint blue accents in the foreground. Add the purple foreground accents with violet, burnt umber, and dots of white and cobalt blue.

48

Step 8 With pure lemon yellow and a flat brush, drybrush some yellow in the canopy of leaves. Using a round brush and white with dots of lemon yellow and light green, paint the highlights in the foliage. With a flat brush, drybrush parts of the branches and the lightest highlights in the foreground with a mixture of white and dots of lemon yellow and crimson. Finally, create a mixture of burnt umber, violet, and light green and use a round brush to paint outlines around the tree trunk, branches, and rooftops. You'll want to water down this mix slightly so that the paint flows freely from your brush.

Mont Sainte-Victoire

"Here on the edge of the river, the motifs are very plentiful, the same subject seen from a different angle gives a subject of the highest interest and so varied that I think I could be occupied for months without changing my place, simply bending a little more to the right or left." —Paul Cézanne*

Transfer the sketch on page 88!

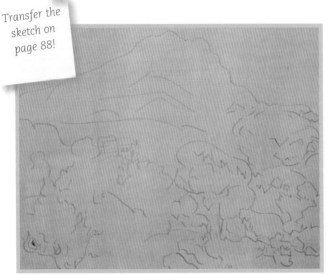

Step 1 Start by creating an underpainting with a wash of yellow ochre. Use a flat brush and repeat this step if necessary to get a nice, even tone.

Step 2 Next paint the sky with a mixture of white, violet, a bit of cobalt blue, and a dot of burnt umber. Use a round brush and paint this area with a lot of energetic expression—the sky should look alive! Add a bit more white to the sky mix to paint the lighter areas of the sky, allowing both colors to blend together in some places.

Step 3 Now paint the darker parts of the sky with a mix of cobalt blue, violet, white, and a dot of burnt umber. With a mixture of cobalt blue and burnt umber, paint the very dark areas of the sky. Now start painting the warm colors of the mountain by mixing white with some yellow ochre and a bit of violet and crimson. Keep this mix on your palette for later steps. Now touch in the second round of warm tones with a mix of white, a little yellow ochre, and a dot of crimson. Keep this mix on your palette as well.

* Chipp, Herschel B. *Theories of Modern Art*. Los Angeles: University of California Press, 1968, 22.

Step 4 Mix white with violet and a dot of red and start painting the light purple areas of the mountain. Then create a darker purple mix with less white, violet, and a dot of crimson, and touch this darker color in. Blend these colors together where they meet, and add more of the two mixes from the last step for additional blending. If you get confused, just follow the colors you see here.

Step 5 Paint all of the very dark areas of the mountain with a mix of violet, a little burnt umber, and a dot of white. Add texture with quick, short strokes. Create a mix of cobalt blue with some violet and white to paint the blue tones that appear throughout the mountain, blending them where they meet other colors. Paint the dark yellow parts of the foreground with a mix of yellow ochre, a little white, and a dot of burnt umber, blending as you paint.

51

Step 6 Next paint all of the dark orange areas of the foreground with a mix of yellow ochre, crimson, a little yellow, and a dot of burnt umber. Then add some of this mix into the mountain. With a mix of yellow, crimson, a little yellow ochre, and a dot of burnt umber, paint the lighter areas of orange in the foreground, blending it with the previous colors. Now mix yellow and green and paint all of the bright green areas in the foreground.

Step 7 Paint the lighter shrubbery with a mix of yellow and green, blending it into the previously applied bright green. Using yellow, burnt umber, and a bit of white, add some of the highlights throughout the landscape. Next paint the blue accents in the shrubbery with cobalt and white using a round brush and quick, sketchy strokes.

Project based on *Mont Sainte-Victoire* (1900) by Paul Cézanne.

Step 8 Remember to keep your brushstrokes loose, even in this final stage of the painting! Using a flat brush and yellow paint, drybrush within the canopy of leaves. Create a mix of white with a dot of yellow and green, and use a round brush to highlight the foliage. Using white mixed with a dot of red and yellow, highlight the mound of earth in the foreground and a few tree limbs. Now create a watered-down mix of equal parts violet, green, and burnt umber. Use this to outline the tree trunks, branches, and rooftops. Create a thicker mix of violet, green, and burnt umber. Add the last of the dark accents you see in the painting, including the outlines of the mountain and houses as well as the dark patches in the foliage.

Still Life with Milk Jug and Fruit

"...Nature reveals herself to me in very complex forms; and the progress needed is incessant. One must see one's model correctly and experience it in the right way; and furthermore express oneself forcibly and with distinction." —Paul Cézanne*

Transfer the sketch on page 89!

Step 1 Start by creating an underpainting with a wash of yellow ochre mixed with a little burnt umber. Use a flat brush and repeat if necessary to get an even tone.

Step 2 Paint the darkest parts of the curtain, wine glass, doorknob, fruit dish, and kettle with a round brush and a mix of burnt umber, violet, and green. Then mix yellow ochre, a little yellow, and a bit of crimson and burnt umber to paint the orange part of the wall and the accents on the table, blending the colors as you go.

Step 3 Paint the slightly lighter shade of the curtains with a mix of burnt umber, a little yellow ochre, and a dot of crimson, blending it with the previous color. Then use the same mix to blend in some shadows under the table ledge and the fruit dish. Mix white with a little violet, yellow ochre, and a dot of burnt umber, and paint the rest of the wall as shown. Add this lavender color to areas of the dish, kettle, and wine glass, and keep this mixture on your palette for later steps. Create a new mix with the same colors and a little green and yellow and use it to accent the wall, dish, kettle, and wine glass. Blend in some of the same mix to the curtains, re-wetting the paint for smooth blends.

* Chipp, Herschel B. *Theories of Modern Art.* Los Angeles: University of California Press, 1968, 19.

Step 4 Next paint the blue accents on the wall, wine glass, and dish with some of the lavender mix from step 3, cobalt blue, and a dot of burnt umber. Then paint the dark shadows on the orange part of the wall and the lines on the violet part of the wall and around the kettle with a round brush and the lavender mix from step 3, adding a little cobalt blue and a dot of burnt umber. Mix a little white into yellow ochre and paint the light areas of the table, blending this with the table mix from step 2.

Step 5 Mix white with dots of yellow ochre and burnt umber and paint some light neutrals on the table, kettle, and dish as shown. Mix white with a little yellow ochre and burnt umber plus a dot of violet to paint more neutrals on the tabletop. This will help give the painting depth and variation. Adding dots of crimson and white to violet, paint the purple shadows on the kettle, dish, wine glass, and tabletop. Then add violet accents to the curtains with the same mix.

Step 6 Paint the shadows under the fruit and dish with violet, a little burnt umber, and a dot of white, blending as you go. Use the drybrush technique on the table edges for texture. Make a watery mix of violet and crimson with a dot of burnt umber, and use a round brush to paint the outlines of the fruit. Using a mix of crimson with a little yellow and a dot of burnt umber, paint the red of the fruit. Drybrush this mix for the right side of the table and the shadows inside the dish.

Step 7 Paint the orange of the fruit with yellow and a little crimson, and then let this dry. With a mix of crimson, yellow, and a dot of burnt umber, paint darker areas of the fruit as shown. Soften the outlines by painting around the fruit with the same mix. Add some darker areas to the fruit with a mix of a little burnt umber, crimson, yellow, and a dot of violet. Add dots of burnt umber and violet to yellow ochre to accent the kettle and the orange wall.

Project based on *Still Life with Milk Jug and Fruit* (1900) by Paul Cézanne.

Step 8 Next add a dot of yellow ochre to white to paint the white areas of the kettle and dish with a round brush. Drybrush the white mixture over some of the previously painted colorful shadows, and then paint a highlight on the piece of fruit in the foreground. Paint the green areas of the kettle with a mix of green and yellow ochre, and add hints of pure cobalt blue in the shadows of the dish. Paint the yellow highlights on the oranges with pure yellow. Finally, paint the brownish-red accents in the curtains with a mixture of burnt umber and crimson.

Paint Like an Expressionist!

Started in the early 1900s, *Expressionism* is a style of art that focuses on expressing feelings and moods. As a result, Expressionist paintings have exaggerated colors and shapes that aren't always realistic or true to life. Within this art movement, a Russian painter named Wassily Kandinsky created paintings made up of unrecognizable forms. He used abstract lines and shapes along with vivid colors to express the emotion of a subject. During his lifetime, Kandinsky created one of the world's most exciting collections of abstract art!

Turn to page 60 to paint this Expressionist masterpiece!

Playing with Emotion

Using Color to Show Mood

You might be surprised at how much color can influence emotion! Colors are often talked about in terms of temperature, since they create either a sense of warmth or coolness when you look at them. Reds, yellows, and oranges are warm. Blues, greens, and purples are cool. And warm and cool colors produce different moods: Warm colors are upbeat and exciting, while cool colors are peaceful and soothing. Painting the same subject in warm and in cool colors will produce two entirely different "feelings," as shown in the images below.

 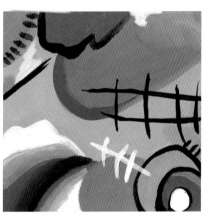

Making Music with Paint

You'd think that painting shapes and lines would result in a boring, stiff image, like the one shown below at left. But Expressionist painter Kandinsky had a way of making the elements of the painting seem to interact with each other and "dance" around the canvas, as though he were painting music. And Kandinsky even named his art as you would name a song, using words like *improvisation* and *composition* to title his artwork. See how the playful arrangement of forms makes the image on the right "feel" like music?

The Life of Wassily Kandinsky
(1866–1943)

Wassily Kandinsky was born in Moscow, Russia, in 1866. A very talented youth, he played both cello and violin, and he excelled in school.

As an adult, Kandinsky studied and taught law. But in 1895, he entered the art world, inspired by French Impressionist paintings. (See pages 14–29.) During the next four years, he attended the Academy of Fine Arts in Germany. And it took only a few years after leaving the academy for Kandinsky to become a successful painter—he even helped form an Expressionist painters' group called *Der Blaue Reiter* (which means "The Blue Rider"). Kandinsky also wrote a book about abstract painting, which involves painting objects in a way that completely ignores how they look in real life.

As Kandinsky grew older, his style became more and more abstract. He passed away in Neuilly, France, in 1944.

Squares with Concentric Circles

"There is no must in art because art is free." —Kandinsky

Transfer the sketch on page 90!

Step 1 Before you begin painting, think of the sketch as a general guide for your design, not an exact pattern to follow. Expressionism is about emotion, so paint freely and loosely! Start by applying thin washes of color, made by mixing your paint with a lot of water. And—if you choose—you can copy the color pattern shown here.

Step 2 Continue filling in all the different sections with thin applications of color. Leave areas unpainted only where you will later add white. As you paint, don't worry about making each circle perfectly round—part of this painting's "feeling" comes from the variety of colors and irregular shapes!

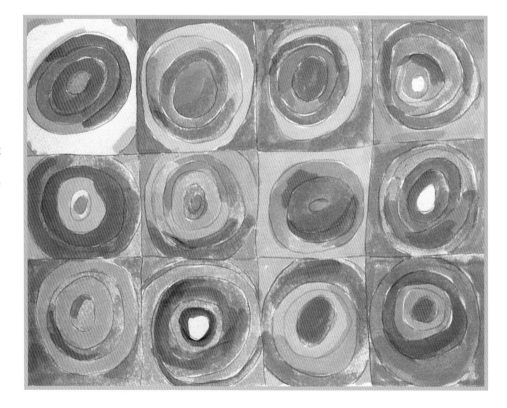

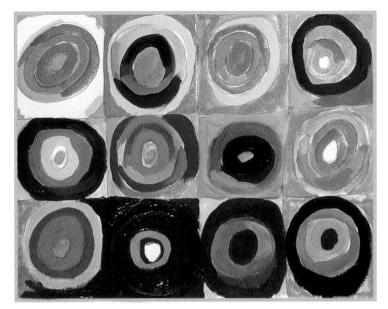

Step 3 Now that you've established all the areas of color, begin applying thicker layers of paint. Stroke in a curving motion that follows the shape of each circle. Within some rings of color, try blending in another color—such as yellow into crimson—as you paint, giving the circles some dimension.

Step 4 When you've finished, check to make sure that each square has a good balance of colors, as well as darks and lights. Then complete your lively Expressionist masterpiece with any last bold, thick strokes of paint!

Paint Like a Cubist!

Artists from the *Cubist* movement had a unique way of painting the world around them. Although you can look at a Cubist painting and figure out what the subject is, it won't look exactly as it does in life. Cubists used a lot of lines and large shapes to make up the objects in their paintings, changing the subjects' appearance. This popular style of painting also shows different surfaces of an object at the same time—for example, the viewer can see the front, sides, and inside of an object all at once. Artist Pablo Picasso developed cubism along with a fellow painter named Georges Braque. Together they gave us a brand new way to look at the world!

Turn to page 64 to paint your own masterpiece in the style of a Cubist!

Playing with Multiple Perspectives

Finding Shapes

Cubists often painted their subjects using simple shapes and flat areas of color. To imitate their style, look at an object near you and try to find the different general shapes within it, such as ovals, rectangles, or even rounded squares. Now look at the pictures below and see how you can take a plain guitar and exaggerate its shapes. (Notice that the handle of the guitar is now a simple rectangle.) You can still recognize the object on the right as a guitar, but the basic shapes and bold outlines give it a flat quality.

Combining Viewpoints

Cubist-style paintings often show an object from several different angles. This way of "seeing" the object is impossible in real life, but Cubists managed to make it happen on canvas. They did this by creating paintings that look as though everything has been pressed flat against the canvas—and sometimes they painted objects as if they were taken apart like a puzzle. When you look at the pictures below, notice that the vase on the left is painted whole, as you would see it. The vase on the right is painted so you can see almost every part of it at the same time!

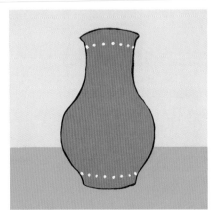

Famous Cubist Painters

The most well-known Cubist—Pablo Picasso—was born in Malaga, Spain, on October 25, 1881. His father, José Ruiz, taught painting, so Picasso discovered art at an early age—he made his first paintings at age 10! His parents recognized his talent and encouraged him to continue drawing and painting in school. After his schooling, he moved to Paris to study the work of famous painters—and he eventually became one himself! Throughout his life, Picasso experimented with many ways of artistic expression. By the time he passed away in 1973, Picasso had participated in sculpture, etching, and graphic art.

Another artist who was key to the development of cubism was named Georges Braque. He was born in Argenteuill-sur-Seine, France, on May 13, 1882. He was introduced to art and painting by working as a house decorator for his father. In 1900, Braque moved to Paris to study art. From this point on, Braque painted in the styles of many art movements—including Impressionism (see page 14), Expressionism (see page 58), and finally cubism. He passed away in 1963.

Cubist Cat

"Good taste is the enemy of creativity." —Pablo Picasso

Step 1 Apply a wash of burnt umber over the work surface. This color will set the stage for neutral colors, which were commonly used by Cubists. After this dries, block in a few areas of the background. In the spirit of the later phase of cubism (called "synthetic cubism"), stick with flat shapes of color. Fill in the triangle at top right with pure burnt umber and the ceiling with a mix of white, burnt umber, and yellow. For the reddish brown areas, use crimson, burnt umber, and dabs of cobalt blue and yellow. Save a bit of this for the next step!

Transfer the sketch on page 91!

Step 2 Create the yellow background shape (at far right) by mixing yellow and a dab of the reddish-brown mix from the last step. This will soften the yellow and help it tie in with the other colors of the background.

Step 3 Now build up the darker colors with thicker layers of paint. Mix burnt umber, yellow, and white to create the light brown in the background. For the darkest color of the cat, mix cobalt blue with burnt umber and a little white. Then apply pure yellow to add color to the dark yellow areas of the cat's chest and ear.

64

Step 4 For the final step, carefully add black to areas as shown. If your paint is too thick to make neat lines, thin it with a little bit of water and apply a few coats. This last step will really help the piece pop!

Paint Like a Pop Artist!

Pop Art first "popped up" in England in the 1950s and came to the United States in the 1960s. Pop Art is based on the belief that commercial art (illustrations and designs used in magazines and ads) is just as respectable as fine art (traditional drawings, paintings, and sculptures). Headed in the United States by artists Andy Warhol, Roy Lichtenstein, and Jasper Johns (among others), Pop Art is known for its bright, attention-grabbing colors and everyday subject matter, such as soup cans, comics, or shoes. And because it is so strongly linked with advertisement, Pop Art appeals to "popular culture" by using trendy or familiar subjects (including famous people) in addition to eye-catching simplicity and repetition.

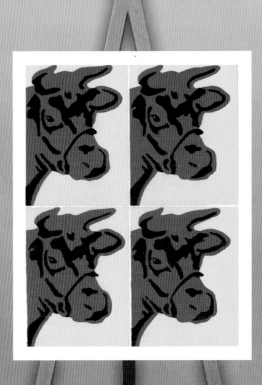

Turn to page 68 to paint this Pop Art masterpiece!

Playing with the Commercial

Creating a Silkscreen Effect

Andy Warhol's most famous pieces of art are made through a process called "silkscreening." With silkscreening, an image is created by applying ink to paper or canvas though a screen. Silkscreening is not a perfect way to reproduce an image because the ink bleeds and blots differently on each print. But these "faults" are part of the appeal of silkscreened artwork, as they make each piece unique. To transform an ordinary painting of an ice cream cone (below left) into one that looks like a silkscreened reproduction (below right), paint the ice cream cone with flat color; then simplify the shadows, making them large, black areas.

Copying the Comic Strip Technique

A form of art that is reproduced in the masses in newspapers and books, comic strips are treated as throwaway entertainment. But the pop movement regards this kind of art as fine art as well, blurring the line between a comic strip picture and—let's say—a Rembrandt. To create this comic strip look in your own painting, follow the technique of Pop Artist Roy Lichtenstein by using expressive black lines and round dots of color (called "Ben Day dots")—just like a newspaper printer!

The Life of Andy Warhol
(1928–1987)

This famous Pop Artist was born in Pittsburgh, Pennsylvania, on August 6, 1928. He graduated from high school in 1945 and then attended the Carnegie Institute of Technology in Pittsburgh. After earning a degree in pictorial design, Warhol moved to New York, where he worked as a commercial artist. There he made a name for himself through his successful shoe advertisements, magazine illustrations, and store window arrangements.

Warhol created images that the public loved, including Coke bottles, portraits of famous people, and cans of Campbell's soup. As the popularity of his art grew, Warhol became famous as a fine artist. In 1962, Warhol's success and the demand for his work resulted in his starting an art studio of his own—called "The Factory"—where he hired artists to help him reproduce his artwork.

Warhol continued creating art until his death in 1987. His images continue to influence both fine art and commercial art today.

Cow Wallpaper

"Isn't life just a series of images that change as they repeat themselves?" —Andy Warhol

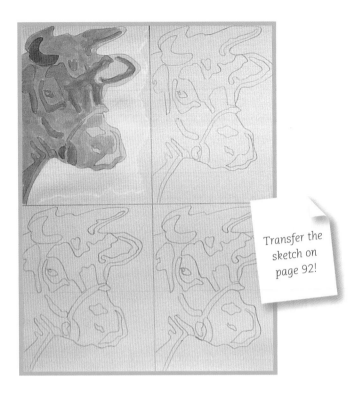

Transfer the sketch on page 92!

Step 1 Start with thin washes of color so that later you can easily paint over mistakes with thicker layers of paint. For the background wash, use yellow paint and water. Then mix white and crimson with some water to paint the cow's pink face. For the shadows, mix a dot of black with water to create gray.

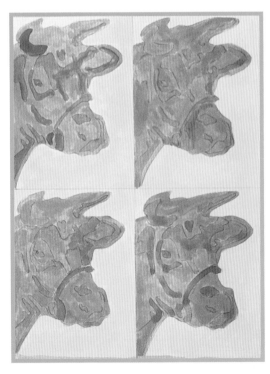

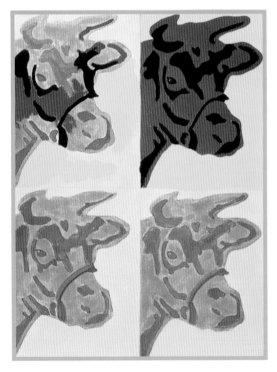

Step 2 Fill in all the remaining areas of the sketch with washes of color. Now you have a clear map for defining the shadows in the faces.

Step 3 Next apply thicker layers of paint. Use pure black paint mixed with a few drops of water to fill in the shadows. Use pure yellow mixed with a few drops of water for the background. For the hot pink color of the cow's face, mix white with a dot of crimson and a dot of yellow. (Take care to not use too much crimson—this color goes a long way!)

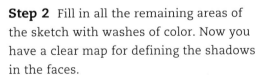

Project based on *Cow Wallpaper* (1966) by Andy Warhol. © 2010 The Andy Warhol Foundation for the Visual Arts / Artists Rights Society (ARS), New York

Step 4 Finish the painting by filling in all the remaining areas with thick paint. Don't worry if all the cow portraits aren't exactly alike—just as with silkscreening, each image will be unique!

Paint Like a Dada Artist!

The *Dada* art movement began during the tragedies of World War I. Because no one could understand how the modern world could allow such a horrible war to happen, many people struggled to find meaning in art. Dadaists challenged traditional art by creating artwork that made people stop and think, sculpting and painting images that challenged the traditional concept of art. For example, Marcel Duchamp, a French Dada artist, painted a mustache and goatee onto a postcard reproduction of the Mona Lisa and presented it as art! Although some thought it a disgrace to the masterpiece, the mustached Mona Lisa served its purpose and had everyone asking an important question: "What is art?"

Turn to page 72 to paint your own masterpiece in the style of a Dadaist!

Playing with Tradition

What Is Art?

For Dada artists, traditional ideas about art were thrown out the window. These artists considered their work "anti-art" and themselves "non-artists." For Dadaists, the purpose of art was not to create objects of beauty—instead art was a way to comment on society. For example, you can transform a traditional portrait of a farmer (below left) into Dada non-art by adding a pig's nose to the farmer's face. To a Dadaist, this might be meant as a comment on the farmer's own animal nature—or a remark about animal rights or abuses.

Viewing the World Differently

There were a few Dada artists who branched out into new and different media and techniques—for example, Hannah Höck created her artwork out of newspaper and magazine clippings, which she used to make collages. But most Dada artists used traditional art techniques to reflect their unique way of seeing the world and the objects within it. Whereas a traditional artist might see a bicycle and want to paint the entire piece of machinery (below left), the Dada artist was more likely to see and be interested in the mechanical aspect of the subject, painting a closeup of the bike's chain and wheel spokes (below right).

Famous Dada Artists

One of the most important figures of the Dada movement was Marcel Duchamp, who was born on July 28, 1887, in Blainville, France. He moved to Paris in 1904 to study art, where he became interested in both fauvism and cubism. However, Duchamp found his niche in the art world with Dada art, providing some incredibly unique pieces of "anti-art." He often added his signature and completely unrelated titles to ready-made objects, like bottle racks and snow shovels, and put them in art exhibits. Perhaps his most well-known piece is *Fountain,* which is a toilet that he signed with a fake name and exhibited as a work of art!

Other famous Dada artists include Jean (Hans) Arp of France, who invented a new form of collage by simply dropping cut pieces of paper onto canvas; Man Ray of the United States, who created cameraless prints by placing objects on photographic paper and exposing them to light; and Max Ernst of Germany, who painted human figures composed of pieces of machinery.

Dada Mona Lisa

"I don't believe in art. I believe in artists." —Marcel Duchamp

Transfer the sketch on page 93!

Step 1 Begin with the sky, applying a light wash of phthalo blue mixed with yellow and a little burnt umber. Then fill in the figure's hair with a thin wash of burnt umber. For the skin and sleeve, use a mix of yellow with a dot of burnt umber. Next add grays to the hat and the bottom of the paper.

Step 2 Wash over the skin with white mixed with a dot of crimson and a little phthalo blue, a little yellow, and a little burnt umber. For sleeve shadows, mix yellow with a dot of burnt umber and a dot of black. The purples are a mix of black, a little phthalo blue, and a little white.

Step 3 Now build up the darks by adding thicker, darker applications of the same colors, blending as you work. Even though their subject matter broke with tradition, Dadaists still followed traditional painting methods and techniques! Mix a dot of white into black for the dark color of the lower background; apply this color to the rings of the coonskin cap as well.

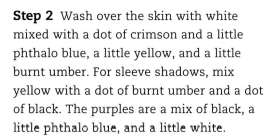

Step 4 To create the fur of the coonskin cap, apply a light purple mix using short brushstrokes, letting some of the darker color show through. Next paint over the skin using white mixed with a dot of crimson and a little phthalo blue, a little yellow, and a little burnt umber. Paint the cloak mostly black with a dot of white and the hair burnt umber, graduating into black toward the tips. For shadows of the sleeves, use burnt umber with a dot of yellow.

Paint Like a Surrealist!

The *Surrealist* movement took form in Europe just before the 1920s. Born out of the Dada movement (see page 70), Surrealism was about bringing hidden or nonsensical ideas and dreams to life through painting, resulting in images of fantasy rather than reality. The Surrealists created dreamlike scenes that show objects painted realistically but in unreal situations—like the open bud of a red rose floating through the sky or a head sprouting from the ground like a tree. One of the most important figures of this movement was Salvador Dalí, a Spanish artist who made famous the images of melting clocks.

Turn to page 76 to paint a masterpiece in the style of a Surrealist!

Playing with Fantasy

Distorting Reality

Because Surrealist art is composed and created in the mind, artists of this unique movement painted with pure imagination—and without any rules! Surrealists were able to take any real object and change or distort anything about it they wanted, whether it was altering the color of the sky or adding long, thin legs to a normally stout elephant, as you can see in the examples below. The subject in the Surrealist painting is still recognizable—but it is being seen in a new way.

 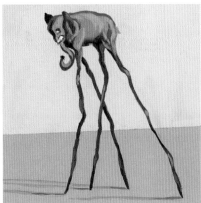

Painting the Absurd

Surrealist painters produced images that weren't just unlikely, they were silly—or absurd! But it wasn't always the *objects* that were absurd; it was the *situation* the objects were painted in that was odd. Ever heard the expression "when pigs fly?" Well, in a Surrealist world, this is possible! Below are two images of a pig. All the objects in both images are real, but the absurdity of the second picture comes in the combination of the elements—wings on a pig and a pig in the sky.

The Life of Salvador Dalí

(1904–1989)

Salvador Dalí was born on May 11, 1904, in the coastal village of Figueres, Spain. In this small fishing town, his parents built him his first art studio, preparing him for his journey to the San Fernando Academy of Fine Arts in Madrid. There his talent was noticed right away, and he began showing his art in exhibitions across Europe and the United States.

Dalí experimented with several styles of painting, including Impressionism (see page 14) and cubism (see page 62). But around 1929, Dalí identified himself as a Surrealist painter. At that time, he also met his wife, Gala Eluard, who provided him with plenty of inspiration and encouragement.

Although Dalí was considered a leader of the Surrealist movement, he was eventually kicked out of the Surrealist group of painters for political reasons. At that point, he began to experiment with other painting styles. By the time of his death in 1989, Dalí had explored a number of artistic paths, including sculpture, jewelry design, film-making, and fiction writing.

Surrealist Rabbit

"Have no fear of perfection—
you'll never reach it." —Dalí

Transfer the sketch on page 94!

Step 1 Tone the background with a wash of phthalo blue.

Step 2 Mix light blue for the sky using white and a bit of phthalo blue. When mixing, always add the darker color to the lighter color in small amounts. Use a flat brush for the sky, switching to a round brush to work around the shapes. Then add a dot of black to the sky mix and create a few shadows. Use pure white to block in the cloud.

Step 3 Mix white and yellow ochre to begin painting the lower ground. Use horizontal strokes and move downward from the straight line (the horizon line). As you move down, blend in pure yellow ochre to create a gradation. Dip your brush in water now and then to keep your paint fluid. Now create the gray sky above the horizon line. Mix white, black, a little violet, and a little burnt umber. Fill in the area with this base mix. Add white along the horizon and blend upward, scumbling here and there to create a stormy sky. Add the mountain with gray, burnt umber, and black.

Step 4 Paint the rabbit using a warm gray mix of white, black, and a dab of burnt umber (keep this color on your palette throughout this step). Separate a glob of this and add a bit of white; then paint the lighter areas of the rabbit. Dab the brush to imitate the fur pattern. Add a touch of red and black to some of the original gray mix, and use this to add shadows to the inner ears and mouth area. Then mix a light pink for the "whites" of the eyes. Mix black and red for the pupils and add white highlights. For the dark underside of the floating ear, add a little black to the original gray mix.

Step 5 To finish the rabbit, mix white with a touch of lemon yellow and highlight areas of the fur. Then dilute the paint and soften the edges of the rabbit against the sky using short, feathery strokes. Use this mix to add some thin whiskers. Using a very light blue mix of white and phthalo blue, drybrush and scumble the edge of every cloud. Add a bit more white to the mix and build on your previous strokes, further softening the edges. Occasionally dip your brush into water so it doesn't dry out.

Templates

These templates include the basic lines for each of the paintings in this book. Make photocopies of the templates so you can use them to transfer the lines to your painting surface (see page 12 for instructions on transferring).

Squares with Concentric Circles

90

Cubist Cat

Project on page 64!

91

Sailboat

Project on page 16!

Project on page 18!

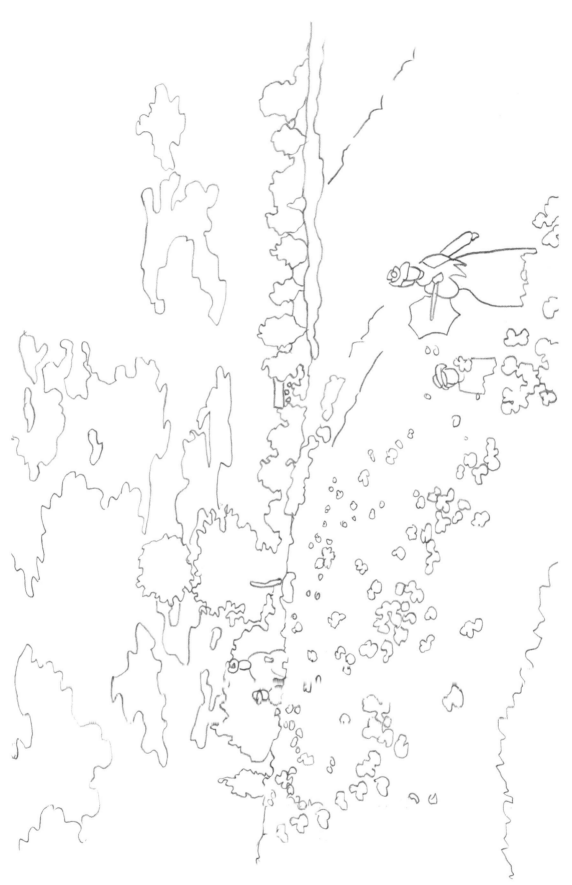

Project on page 26!

Sunflowers

Sunflowers

Project on page 34!

Project on page 38!

Project on page 42!

Project on page 46!

Project on page 50!

Project on page 54!

Project on page 60!

Cubist Cat

Project on page 64!

91

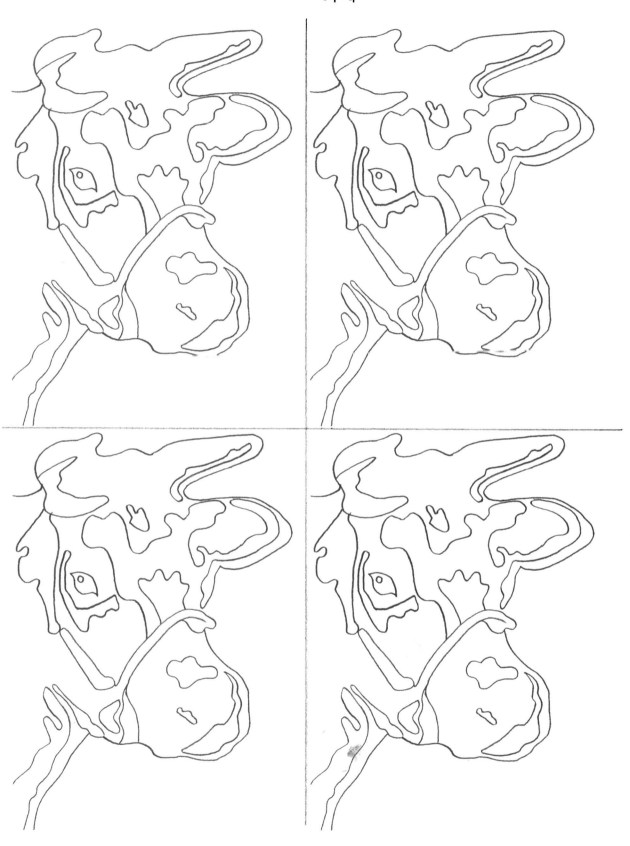

Project on page 68!

Dada Mona Lisa

Project on page 72!

Project on page 76!

Conclusion

I hope you enjoyed exploring
some art history while making your
own masterpieces! Allow this book to be
your starting point for a life-long investigation
of art and your relationship to it. You have
learned some valuable techniques to
help you create great artwork of your own.
There is so much more to learn, so keep painting
and go to your local museums and art galleries.
Art is always better when experienced in person.

Meet the Artist!

Amy Runyen is a mixed media artist and a painter who has shown her fine art work in galleries in the United States, Canada, and Italy. She was a mural artist for the *Envisioning The Future Project* with Judy Chicago. In addition to her fine art career, Amy has authored and illustrated eight how-to-paint books and wrote the art history section for *The Daily Book of Art* from Walter Foster Publishing.

Originally from San Diego, California, Amy attended the Savannah College of Art and Design in Savannah, Georgia, graduating with a BFA in illustration. She has studied figure painting in Florence, Italy, and achieved her MFA in drawing and painting at California State University Long Beach.

Currently, she is an adjunct faculty member in the art departments at various colleges and universities in the greater Los Angeles area and has been a guest lecturer at colleges in Los Angeles and Nevada. She now lives and makes art in South Pasadena with her husband, fellow artist Nathan Rohlander.

31901050395542